# One Mistake-
# Many Problems

Dr. Emmanuel Oduro

authorHOUSE®

AuthorHouse™
1663 Liberty Drive
Bloomington, IN 47403
www.authorhouse.com
Phone: 1-800-839-8640

Published by AuthorHouse   01/31/2015

ISBN: 978-1-4969-6284-3 (sc)
ISBN: 978-1-4969-6309-3 (e)

KJV
Scripture quotations marked KJV are from the Holy Bible, King James
Version (Authorized Version). First published in 1611. Quoted from the KJV
Classic Reference Bible, Copyright © 1983 by The Zondervan Corporation.

NKJV
Scripture quotations marked NKJV are taken from the
New King James Version. Copyright © 1982 by Thomas
Nelson, Inc. Used by permission. All rights reserved.

# Contents

## Dedication

This book is dedicated to my wife Helena and my sons David and Danny who helped in typing most of the materials in this book. Many thanks also go to my wife who also encouraged me to print this book. I thank her for her support and encouragement in putting this book together as well. The Lord blesses all of you.

# Introduction

I titled this book "One Mistake-Many Problems" for several reasons. First of all, I want to explain what is meant by a "mistake." The Concise Oxford Dictionary defines "mistake as an incorrect idea or opinion. A thing incorrectly done or thought."

We all make mistakes. Some of our mistakes are accidental while others are intentional and sinful. There are many mistakes found in the scriptures. In Genesis 3 both Adam and Eve responded to mistakes by shifting the blame to each other after eating the forbidden fruit. Sampson also made a foolish mistake when she revealed the secret of his strength to Delilah. This led to his capture and his eyes gouged out. In the same way our parents made several mistakes by going to satanic agents for solutions to problems they were going through. Some of the mistakes our parents created were by selfish pursuit of their own agenda. They made evil contracts with satanic agents in exchange for something without knowing the consequences. We are now reaping the consequences.

As we read through this book we may be able to understand and know some of the mistakes our parents or we ourselves did which have affected us. The writer explains what we could do to come out of any mistake we might have done knowingly or unknowing that have brought untold hardships in our lives.

# Chapter 1

# The Works of the Devil

"And no wonder Satan himself transforms himself into an angel of light" (2 Corinthians 11:14)

Satan has been described as the father of all lies. Let's closely examine some of his works against the children of God and why he has been described as the father of lies.

## 1. SIN-REBELLION

"And the woman said to the serpent, "We may eat the fruit of the trees of the garden" (Gen 3:2)

Satan deceived man to give the first lie in the Bible that Adam and Eve would not die contrary to what God had said. Satan keeps making believers to lie always. He is described as the Father of lies in John 8:44. Don't allow him and his agents to get you to tell lies. He uses lies to steal our destinies. Resist him from today by telling the truth. Earlier God has told Adam and Eve in Gen 1:28 to:

a. Be fruitful
b. Multiply (1:28)
c. Replenish (1:28)
d. Exercise dominion and not give it to another (Gen 1:28; 2:15)
e. Refrain from eating of the knowledge of good and evil.

The last two were broken through the lies of Satan. Through deception the destinies of Adam and was repackaged. They lost every good thing designed for their destinies.

## 2. WORKS OF DARKNESS

"And have no fellowship with the unfruitful works of darkness, but rather expose them" (Ephesians 5:11).

The enemy makes people go into moral sedition and sex perversion so that he will use those as a stepping stone to interfere into their lives. Live a moral and clean life until you marry that guy or lady you plan to marry. If your fiancé or fiancée entices you to have affairs before marriage don't accept it because it is contrary to the Word of God.

## 3. WORKS OF WICKEDNESS

"Oh, let the wickedness of the wicked come to an end, but establish the just; For the righteous God tests the hearts and minds" (Psalm 7:9).

This Psalm tells us that all the wickedness of the world today is initiated by the devil and we need to pray and stop his activities. The psalmist says in part, "Oh let the wickedness of the wicked come to and end". This will only happen when believers stand up and pray. The wickedness of Absalom and Ahithophel to overthrow David did not happen because King David went to the mountains to pray to avert the evil plot. Prayer, therefore, is the key to stop every evil activity of the devil.

## 4. SPIRITUAL BLINDNESS

"Whose minds the god of this age has blinded, who do not believe, lest the light of the gospel of the glory of Christ, who is the image of God, should shine on them" (2 Corinthians 4:4)

The enemy has blinded the minds of many people including some believers. People claim to be believers and still fornicate, steal, lie, and gossip which is all work of Satan as Paul made it clearly in Galatians 5:19.

## 5. STEALING THE WORD

For the hearts of this people have grown dull. Their ears are hard of hearing, And their eyes they have closed, Lest they should see with their eyes and hear with their ears, Lest they should understand with their hearts and turn, So that I should heal them (Math 5:19).

The enemy steals the Word of God from believers by putting in their thoughts that what they read or hear form the Bible is not true. He will put in your mind that if the word is true that," by his stripes you are healed why then are you still suffering from a certain illness for such a long time. Don't listen to him. He did that to Adam and Eve and they died spiritually. He wants to steal our destiny. It is, important therefore, to renew our mind with the Word of God often.

## 6. TO KILL AND DESTROY

"The thief does not come except to steal, and to kill and to destroy I have come that they may have life, and that they may have it more abundantly" (John 10:10).

In contrast to the thief which is Satan and his agents who take life, Jesus says He has come to give life. The life Jesus gives is abundantly rich and full. It is eternal, yet it begins immediately. Life in Christ is lived on a higher plane because of His overflowing love and guidance.

Jesus plainly tells us in the above scripture that Satan comes to steal, to kill and to destroy. He attacks with any of the above as his aim. For instance, he could steal your joy by stealing the fruit of your womb. If he does not succeed in this area he could kill your child at an early age. We need to resist him so that he does not succeed in any of those areas.

## 7.  SOWING TARES

"but while men slept, his enemy came and sowed tares among the wheat and went his way" (Mathew 13:25).

It was common in the East for enemies to sow tares in the field of those they wish to harm. In India for instance, there were seeds sown among wheat while growing. When they are fully grown, the farmer is unable to differentiate the good ones from bad ones. Both good and bad wheat were allowed to grow until the end of the harvest when the farmer separates the good from bad wheat.

In the physical the enemy does the same to human beings. In our step, he comes to have affair with women to give them sickness or to deposit sickness in their womb to prevent pregnancy.

## 8.  ACCUSING THE BRETHREN

"But the earth helped the woman, and the earth opened its mouth and swallowed up the flood which the dragon had spewed out of his mouth" (Rev.12:16).

Many Bible scholars believe that until this time, Satan had access to go to God. The Book of Job confirms this in Job 1:7 when God asked Satan where had been. He replied that he had been going up and down watching what was happening on Earth.

He is an accuser. He accused Joshua the high priest as recorded in Zechariah 3:1-2. Joshua was the High Priest when the Israelites returned to Jerusalem to rebuild the walls. Satan's accusation against Joshua was accurate. Joshua stood in filthy clothes that are in sin. God showed mercy to him and Israel. God chose to forgive His people in spite of their sin. Satan is always accusing people of their sins before God as in Job Chapter 1.

Satan greatly misunderstands the breadth of God's mercy and forgiveness towards those who believe in Him. Satan will one day be destroyed (Rev 12:10) while everyone who is a believer will be saved (John 3:16).

We can also ask God to remove our clothing of sin and dress us with His goodness. The vision of the Prophet Zechariah shows how we receive God's mercy. We do nothing ourselves. God removes our filthy clothes, and then provides us with fine new clothes, that is; the righteousness and holiness of God Himself.

## 9. HINDER PRAYERS

Then he said to me, "Do not fear, Daniel, for from the first day that you set your heart to understand, and to humble yourself before your God, your words were heard; and I have come because of your words. "But the prince of the kingdom of Persia withstood me twenty-one days; and beholds, Michael, one of the chief princes, came to help me, for I had been left alone there with the kings of Persia. "Now I have come to make you understand what will happen to your people in the latter days, for the vision refers to many days yet to come." When he had spoken such words to me, I turned my face toward the ground and became speechless. And suddenly, one having the likeness of the sons of men touched my lips; then I opened my mouth and spoke, saying to him who stood before me, "My lord, because of the vision my sorrows have overwhelmed me, and I have retained no strength. "For how can this servant of my lord talk with you, my lord? As for me, no strength remains in me now, nor is any breath left in me." Then again, the one having the likeness of a man touched me and strengthened me. And he said, "O man greatly beloved, fear not! Peace be to you; be strong, yes, be strong!" So when he spoke to me I was strengthened, and said, "Let my lord speak, for you have strengthened me." Then he said, "Do you know why I have come to you? And now I must return to fight with the prince of Persia; and when I have gone forth, indeed the prince of Greece will come. "But I will tell you what is noted in the Scripture of Truth. (No one upholds me against these, except Michael your prince.

This is a good example of a prayer request that was delayed by Satan. This did not cause Daniel to give up but rather prayed more until the promised comes to pass. The passage says "I am come for thy word." This phrase indicates that when we pray God hears the exact words we speak and he answers. It is important to be specific in our prayer requests.

God has promised to give to all men what they ask for in prayer if they believe. Over all the governments of this world, Satan has his trusted angels who are responsible to him for carrying out his will in those governments. He seeks to hinder, destroy God's plan regarding world's kingdoms. God also has His trusted angels who carry out His will concerning what he has promised to place in those kingdoms of this planet. This is why there is a war between these two groups of angels in the heaven lies. All wars lost or won on earth are results of wars lost or won by these heavenly armies. Satan's main aim is to defeat the purpose God has for his children. The vision of Daniel tells us that there is a warfare going on between Satan and God's children. Don't give up when you don't receive instant answer to your prayer. There might be a human finger behind your problem. God said we should be fruitful. Why have you married for 7 years and God's command to be fruitful is not seen in the marriage. Stand up and fight because you are more than a conqueror.

## 10. CAUSING SICKNESS AND DISEASES.
### (Matt 9:32-33; 8:28)

"As they went out, behold, they brought to Him a man, mute and demon-possessed. And when the demon was cast out, the mute spoke: and the multitudes marveled, saying, "It was never so seen in Israel". Jesus had power over demonic sicknesses and diseases. The same spirit in Christ is also in us as we become born again. Therefore we have power over any sickness inflicted on us by the devil.

Again, in Mathew 8: 28 Jesus came to the country of the Gergesenes, and met two demon possessed men, coming out of the tombs, exceedingly fierce, so that no one could pass that way.

Gadara was a town which was mostly inhabited by Gentiles according to Biblical scholars. This explains why probably there were herd of pigs. Jews did not raise pigs because they were considered unclean and unfit to eat.

Demon-possessed people are under the control of one or more demons. Demons are fallen angels who joined Satan against God. They are now evil spirits under Satan's control. They assist Satan to tempt people to sin. Whenever they are control by Jesus they loose their destructive powers. In that scripture, the demons recognized Jesus as the son of God but did not want to obey Him. It is only Christ who can destroy the works of the enemy over our lives. These two men lived in the cemetery. A person in his right mind will never do that. They were demon possessed. Christ still heals today. Whatever sickness the enemy puts on children of God, Christ is able to heal us if only we believe.

Jesus really demonstrated His healing power over every sickness as confirms in Acts 10:38 that, Jesus was anointed with the Holy Spirit and with power to set free people who are oppressed by the devil. As a child of God stand on your faith and stop the activities of Satan against God. Demons are now evil spirits under Satan's control. They assist Satan to tempt people to sin. Whenever they are controlled by Jesus, they loose their destructive powers.

In that scripture the demons recognized Jesus as the son of God but did not want to obey Him. It is only Christ who can destroy the works of the enemy over our lives. These two men lived in the cemetery. A person in his right mind will never do that. They were demon possessed. Christ still heals today.

Whatever sickness the enemy puts on children of God, Christ is able to heal us if only we believe. Jesus really demonstrated his healing power over every sickness as confirms in Acts 10:38 that, Jesus was anointed with the Holy Spirit and with power to set free people who were oppressed by the devil. Child of God stand, I challenge to stand on your faith and stop the activities of Satan and his agents against you.

# Chapter 2

# The Mystery of the Human Body

There are 3 important parts of the human body that play very important spiritual role in humankind's destiny. These are:

## A. THE FACE

Face represents glory, God's presence. So when your face is covered spiritually your glory is covered. When your glory is covered many bad things happen to you such as:

- Your helpers will not locate you and help. If you are a woman no man is interested you. When they see you despite your beauty.
- Spirit of error takes over your life. When you are supposed to do something that will benefit you, it

passes you by. What will not benefit you is what you do.

- Evil spirits begin to attack. This is what happened to Saul when the Holy Spirit left him.
- You make wrong decisions because your brain is under attack by forces of darkness (Ps 7:16)
- You don't hear from the Lord (1 Sam 4:21).
- Your star becomes covered or dim.
- Loss of memory you can no longer remember things as you used to.

## B. WHAT MAKES US LOOSE OUR GLORY? (Job 34:29)

1. Sin takes God's glory away from us. This is what happened to Adam and Eve when they sinned in the Garden of Eden. They lost every good plan that God had for them. God had a plan of welfare for that family. We should try to live a clean life.

## SYMPTOMS OF LOST GLORY

"And he said I beseech thee show me thy glory" (Exodus 33:18).

At this point Moses had advanced in age and has accomplished as he expected. He therefore, wanted to know where his glory was. We need to ask God from time to time where our glory is

For us to know that our glory has been stolen, look for the following signs or some of them.

a.  False accusation: People accuse you for what you have not done.

b.  Hatred: People hate you for no apparent reason.

c.  Maltreatment: In any group you are, you receive bad treatment

d.  People direct you blessings to others. You don't get what you deserve.

e.  Cheating: People come to you for help anytime you lend or others borrow from you they refuse to pay.

f.  Rejection: Disappointment is always your portion no matter your efforts. A lady married and divorced six times because her glory has been stolen.

g.  Difficulties: You try your best to work hard every day. In the end somebody comes to enjoy your labor.

## C.  THE FEET

Our feet take us to many places either to do good or evil such as prison, hospital, church or farm. Without feet we become stagnant. Our feet carry us to our destiny for either good or bad. For instance, we read of a man Paul heals from birth at Lystra (Acts 14:8-11). The man relied on people for his daily activities and alms. We could imagine how this man's destiny was seized both physically and spiritual.

The feet are very important spiritually in the following areas:

## 1. Possession: (Joshua 6:12-17, 20)

The children of Israel walked around the wall of Jericho for 7 days to possess the city of Jericho as Joshua was told (Joshua 1:3). Our feet have the ability to possess. Lazarus had to be loosened spiritually and physically in order to go and possess his possession. It is through the feet that we conquer our enemies, get new jobs, get our breakthroughs. When ones feet are bound by Satan his/her destination is failure, disappointments, limitations, hindrances and retrogression. Even though you are born to be a winner you become a beggar in the land of abundance. We need to fight to lose our feet from every kind of bondage.

## 2. Feet washing (John 13:4-5)

Washing your feet symbolize cleansing from any spiritual bondage or contamination. By washing our feet we will be able to reach your destination. Windows of opportunities open to us. When our faces and feet are washed we reach our destination. You possess the gates of your enemies and success becomes your destination. It is my prayer that our feet will never take us to pain, death, and disaster. Only Christ can set us free from any spiritual bondage.

D.  THE HANDS (Eccl 10:18)

**1.  Use of Hands:**

The hands are used to pick items, hold items, grasp, work and touching. The hands are also for doing warfare (Ps 144:1) and for blessing people (Deut 28:12). The hands are also used for working to support our families. Many hands are working from hand to mouth. Why? This is because many hands are tied up spiritually. In Job 1:10-11 the devil confronted God that Job has been blessed by God of everything he has done. The devil went on to say that if God withdraws His protection from Job's life, the picture will be different because the devil will have an opportunity to interfere in Job's handiwork. This tells us that the enemy can interfere in whatever we do with our hands.

2.  The effects of tied hands.

In the spiritual realm, when a person's hands are tied, the person works hard but has nothing to show for it. Failure becomes part and parcel of life. One will work hard but will not enjoy his or her labor. Holding unto something becomes impossible. They work and handover to others to enjoy. Whatever they touch breaks down. You earn wages which do not meet needs. Lack is part and parcel of tied hands. Whatever such people touch breaks down.

3. How can the devil bind our hands spiritually?

The devil is able to bind our hands because of what our ancestors might have done. For instance, in Jeremiah 40:4, the prophet was bound physically in the Babylonian captivity even though he was a prophet. He was physically set free but spiritually he needed freedom.

4. The spiritual importance of blessing hands. (Deut 33:11)

The hands that are spiritually blessed receive the wealth of the wicked and whatever they do is blessed. Jesus' hands were nailed to the cross for our hands as believers to be fruitful and be blessed (John 20:25). Anything contrary to this is interference from the enemy.

**How to be freed.**

We get freedom through all or any of the following means

    a. Be born Again

    b. Be filled with the Holy Spirit

    c. Daily reading the Word of God

d.  Knowing that the devil is defeated

e.  Seek deliverance

f.  Using your spiritual weapons: Jesus' name, His Blood, and God's promises.

Pray this prayer daily to deliver your hands.

**Prayer "I decree and declare that whatever is holding my hands are broken in the name of Jesus. Every spiritual chain, holding my hands and every evil powers tampering with my destiny, receive Holy Ghost fire. Let satanic grave clothes which tie up my hands be broken now in the name of Jesus Christ. Am**en.

# Chapter 3

# The Mystery Of Sacrifice

## A. Definition of sacrifice:

Sacrifice simply means the offering of animals or anything valuable on an altar to a deity. Sacrifice involves the shedding of blood on an altar. It is only blood that empowers or activates an altar.

## B. Reasons for Sacrifices

The reasons for sacrifices include some of the following:

1. For propitiation (satisfying divine anger)
2. For success
3. For healing
4. For progress
5. For good marriage
6. To stop evil occurrences

The above reasons could also be used to make evil sacrifice against somebody. People are going through some problems in lives because our fore fathers have offered sacrifices. We also need to pray to activate God's altar through our giving's. Christ has done the sacrifice for us once and for all. The Blood of Jesus still speaks because blood does not loose its power.

There is power in the blood to reach the highest mountain and to the lowest valley or the abyss when the blood of Jesus touched the Earth, it shook, graves opened, those held captives were released.

Anywhere you were disgraced and humiliated by the blood form evil altars, the blood of the lamb will be you celebrate.

**Origin of Sacrifice**

Sacrifice originated by God immediately Adam and Eve had sin. God made tunics of animals skins for them (Gen 3:21). It was a ritual where the sinner will use the blood or flesh to atone for sins. The provision of the tunic was a symbol that sinful man could come before God without fear of death.

**Cain & Abel's Sacrifices**

God required that humans offered sacrifices to Him. Cain offered the Lord the best part of his harvest but unfortunately it was rejected by the Lord. Abel on the other hand offered the best of his animal which was pleasing to God. Cain killed his brother out jealousy because his harvest sacrifice was not accepted (Gen 4:1-8). In the spiritual realm he who gives the highest dominates. The blood of an animal is higher than that of a farm produce. So Abel's sacrifice forced God to appear.

## Noah's Altar

When Noah left the Ark after it rained for 40 days and nights, his first act was to build an altar to offer sacrifice as required of him (Gen 8:20). This is the reason why God asked him to take into the Ark every clean animal acceptable to God by sevens a male and a female (Gen 7:2).

## Abraham's sacrifice

Abraham regularly worshipped God by offering sacrifices to Him. (Gen 12:7, 13:4, 18). What is important for us to note is that God required the people to bring the best of their substance and to present it to the Lord in a specific way.

## There were three central ideas for sacrifices

    a.  Consecration: This means to set apart or dedicate to the service of a deity or to make, an object of honor.

b. Expiation: This means covering of sins

c. Propiation: This means satisfying Devine anger by shedding innocent blood. The purpose of each sacrifice was that God demanded the shedding of innocent blood for the covering of man's sins.

The principle of sacrifice has not been abolished in the New Testament. God continues to require sacrifices from his children such sacrifice of worship, thanksgiving, and righteousness (Ps 4:5). God used sacrifices to prepare His people for the Messiah's ultimate sacrifice.

**The Meaning of a Sacrifice**

Sacrifice is defined as the offering of an animal, plant, food, drink or human life to a deity as propitiation. It is the surrender or destruction of something prized or desirable for the sake of something considered as having a high or more pressing claim.

**Old Testament Sacrifices**

There were all kinds of sacrifices in the Old Testament. Let's briefly throw light on them. They include:

**Burnt Offering**

This involved the killing of a male animal which was wholly consumed by fire. The animal was killed. The priest then collected the blood and sprinkled it around the altar (Num 28:1-8). The burning of the animal symbolized the worshippers' desire to be purged of sinful acts.

## Grain Offering (Lev 2)

The purpose of the grain offering was similar to that of burnt offering. The grain was brought to the priest who will then throw a portion of it into the fire. This process was accompanied by the burning of incense.

## Peace Offering (Lev 3)

This was a ritual meal. It was shared with God, the priests, and other worshippers. The people of Israel were always required to offer peace offering before going to a war.

## Voluntary animal offering (Gen 31:53-55)

This was a sacrifice that expressed praise to God and fellowship with others. We see this kind of fellowship between Jacob and Laban in Genesis (31:53-55).

## Sin Offering (Lev 4:5-12)

This was a goat or sheep offering to make atonement for sins for which restitution was not possible. This kind of offering was made for lesser or unintentional offences.

Two young doves or pigeons were also used in place of a sheep or goat if one cannot afford a goat or sheep.

These sacrifices offered by Israel were to teach them the following:

- How to fulfill their priestly call. Israel was a nation redeemed and established as a kingdom of priests and a nation under the Law of Moses.
- To teach them how to fulfill their priestly call
- To teach them also that God must be approach by the sacrificed offerings through a priest
- To teach them also that God must be approached by the sacrificial offering through a priest
- To purify the nation from unseemliness
- As a reminder that the Holy God required the costly gift of life in blood. As stated in Heb 9:22 "without shedding of blood there is no remission of sin"

It was illegal for anyone else to do the offering other than the priests according to Leviticus 17:1-4. Therefore, Aaron and his sons were set apart to perform the functions of a high priest and priests respectively.

Thanks to Christ Jesus who has come to put an end to blood sacrifice once and forever. This is because in the realm of the spirit the highest blood wins. The blood of Jesus supersedes any other blood.

## Biblical Illustrations of sacrifices

### 1. Noah's Sacrifice (Gen 8:20-22)

When Noah and his children came out of the Ark he raised and altar and sacrificed to the Lord. The spirit of the Lord came down and promised never to use water to destroy the Earth again.

### 2. Israel's sacrifice (Exodus 12:1-14)

When the children of Israel were in bondage for about 400yrs, God sent Moses to deliver them. God used Moses to perform nine miracles but the children of Israel were not set free. When the children of Israel sacrificed a lamb and used the blood on their door posts. God's spirit immediately descended in Egypt that night to execute judgment on the first born of all Egyptians including animals. The Lord said, "When I see the blood I will pass over (Exodus11:13).

In order words, God said, the only thing that will exempt anyone from His anger was blood sacrifice.

The angel of the Lord passed through the Land that night and killed the entire first born of Egypt both man and beasts. In the houses of the Israelites, nobody died because of the sacrifice and blood on their door posts.

When God enters our affairs there is freedom, prosperity and progress which prayers, fasting and deliverance could not achieve. When the Blood of Jesus speaks it overpowers every power. Surely, our sacrifices disarm all demonic powers. Today believers don't sacrifice as seen in the Old Testament but our giving activates the Blood of Jesus to speak on our behalf.

### 3. Prophet Elijah's sacrifice (2 King 18:30-39)

A time came when Israelites' faith was between two opinions. Either to serve the true God or serve idols which God had warned them before they arrived in the Promised Land. A time came when they could not face certain issues they were going through in life. This happens in the life of everyone today which forces people to choose solutions from strange gods.

In the above scripture, Elijah proved to the Israelites that the God of Abraham is the same yesterday, today and forever. no matter the challenges we face we still need to hold unto him.

### 4. Abraham's Sacrifice (Gen 15:7-18)

Abraham's sacrifice made God to enter into a covenant with him and told him the future of his children. Whenever a sacrifice comes on God's altar, God shows up and speaks. For instance, when Abraham offered Isaac on Mount Moriah, the presence of the Lord appeared and swore by Him to bless Abraham and multiply his seed.

Every Christian is a beneficiary of the covenant blessings of Abraham.

## 5.  Solomon's Sacrifice (2 Chronicle 1:6-12)

When God saw 1000 bulls of sacrifice from Solomon, He appeared to him in a dream and asked him what he wanted. He asked for wisdom which God granted. These two things bring down God's presence to us.

a.  Sacrifice on God's altar

b.  Praise and worship

When God presence comes, He fights those who oppose our progress, make our enemies to drink their own blood. The secret is that a sacrifice forces all spiritual laws into motion.

## 6.  Samuel's Sacrifice (1 Sam 7:7-14)

There was a battle between Israel and the Philistines Samuel offered sacrifice to God. God thundered against the Philistines and ended the battle. In order, for God fights for you, take something valuable such as a car, property or big money and give to the Lord.

Many people are struggling in life because somebody in the family out of ignorance sacrificed to an altar of Satan. We also need to change the situation through sacrifices. Sacrifices, therefore, attract God's presence to fight for you. For God to fight our battles we need to offer substantial sacrifices on God's altar.

He summoned the 450 prophets of Baal to a contest at Mount Carmel to end the contradictions. The false prophets took the challenge to prove that Baal us powerful than the God of Israel. The prophets of Baal shouted from morning until the evening sacrifice which was around 3pm. Nothing happened.

Elijah prepared his new altar (2 King 18:3-33) by destroying that of the Baal prophets. He put sacrifice on the altar and called on the God of Abraham, Isaac and Jacob and said, "Let it be known this day…. Hear me, oh Lord. Hear me, that this people may know that thou are the Lord." Immediately, he finished talking fire came form heaven to devour the burnt sacrifice along with the water and the 12 stones. Our God is a consuming fire.

God answered immediately not because of Elijah's prayer but the secret was his new altar and his new sacrifice God simply came down by fire to consume the sacrifice. This ended the controversy of who was the true God.

Many believers call on the same God that answer by fire but nothing happens. Why? The absolute truth is that, God will only show up when there is sacrifice on his altar. If we need to end the contradictions in our lives, we need to build new altars and sacrifice on them. We need to give to God an amount that supersedes what has been sacrifice against us. We will see that God will answer by fire. This is what Gideon was asked to do in the book of Judges 6.

As a New Testament believer, we don't sacrifice animals any longer. Christ has done the sacrifice once and for all. All we need to do is to constantly give to God's altar to activate the Blood of Jesus because blood does not die. The Blood of Jesus will speak for you as a believer.

### 7. David's Sacrifice (2 Sam 24:12-25)

David had counted the people of Israel contrary to the will of God which did not please God. God was angry with David and wanted to punish Israel. David prayed to God for mercy. God gave him three options of punishments to choose from. The punishments were:

a.  7 yrs of famine
b.  Fleeing 3 months before your enemies
c.  Pestilence in Israel for 3 days


David chose the last of the three because he knows God to be a merciful God. Men have no mercy and so chose the last option. 70,000 men died of the plague. This pestilence should have lasted much longer. David did not want to be in the hands of a man again because of the experience he had with Saul for years and his flight from Absalom, his own son.

The plague started in the morning and continued for 3 days and 3 nights throughout the whole land of Israel. The angel was ready for a special judgment on Jerusalem and God commanded the angel to stop. Jerusalem was God's beloved city which was chosen for His headquarter on earth and a place to live and operate through His chosen people. "It is enough, stay now your hand, God said".

David prayed directly to God. This tells us that we don't need to go through anyone to speak to God other than Christ Jesus.

David's second repentance was that he was willing to take the blame and suffering if God will only spare the innocent 70,000 who people died because one person's mistake. Many people die or go through certain problems that they did nothing to deserve those punishments because of one person's mistake.

Again, God sent the Prophet Gad to David to make a sacrifice to atone for his sin and to turn the wrath of God away. David went to Araunah to ask for land to raise an altar there to sacrifice as God has commanded through the prophet. Araunah was willing to give the threshing floor for free but he refused and paid 50 shekels of silver for the land. 50 shekels would be only $32 at 64 cents a shekel according to historical records. According to chronicle 21:25, David bought the land for 600 shekels of gold. Historical records show that the entire land measures about 8 acres and cost $5,817 in our today's currency. This is the land that Solomon built the first Temple according to 2 Chronicle 3:1-2.

When David built the altar and offered burnt and peace offerings. God changed His mind and stopped the plague. If God can stop what he plans to do, He can also stop anything the devil plans illegally against God's children. The untimely death, divorce, sickness, bareness, lack, poverty, and all those satanic attacks can be stopped through constant sacrifices; that are through sacrificial giving. David said, he will not give to God that costs him nothing. Let's give to God something substantial to stop whatever we are going through in life.

A sacrifice is that which is not convenient for you to release or to let go as Abraham was about to do concerning Isaac, his only son. Sacrifice causes you pain to release or inconvenient to your budget. If it does not cost you anything then it is not a sacrifice. Take a great sacrifice to end the bareness, poverty, lack in your life and family. Let's give up something very important and precious because the future is greater than the present. The devil would not allow us to sacrifice because when we do that he looses the battle. Let's stop him with our valuable sacrifices. There are certain things our prayers and fasting cannot do but our sacrifices on God's altar will stop the voice of sacrifice of our fathers on evil altars which are fighting us.

Since our future is greater than our present. Let's take the most precious things we have and drop it on God's altar and stop the madness of Satan and his agents against us. This is the only way we can have ceaseless testimonies.

## EFFECTS OF EVIL SACRIFICES

### A. Curses

There are different kinds of curses mention in Deuteronomy 28:15ff

When someone is under a curse things go very rough. Whatever you lay your hands on to do does not progress. A curse stays in a family for generations- second, third and fourth generations. Curses work in many areas of people's lives including financial curse, marital curse, premature death and chronic or incurable sicknesses.

### B. Prayer Life

If a family is affected by demonic sacrifice, it is difficult to pray. Your prayers are also hindered. In such a situation, you need the Holy Spirit assistance. Pray to be filled with the Holy Spirit. It is only through the Holy Spirit's help that we can pray and get results.

## C. Diseases

God told the people of Israel that if they disobey Him as they go to the Promised Land, He will put incurable diseases on them. Society disobedience to God has brought incurable diseases such as HIV, Ebola and caner.

## D. Occult Covenants

In the spirit world covenants are legal contracts and they are binding until broken by the Blood of Jesus Christ. These evil covenants could affect our relationship with God until they are destroyed though deliverance payers.

## E. Evil Dreams

There are dreams that come from satanic agents to attack us in our dreams. In evil dreams, you experience all kinds of attacks such as animals chasing us. Satanic power could enter any animal and attack us through our dreams. Every satanic attack though a dream always leaves a mark if not immediately destroy through prayer. I know of a Christian sister who was bitten by snake in a dream. In three days' time, the hand got swollen. Demons are spirits and they operate through either human beings or animals to accomplish an assignment. That is why we see animals chasing us in our dream or having affairs in a dream with someone. The following are some of the effects of satanic attacks in dreams.

**Other effects include:**
1. Leaving a vagabond Life
2. unproductive life
3. Caged destiny
4. Evil soul ties
5. Unprofitable life
6. Premature death
7. Destiny demotion
8. Unhappy marriage//Late marriage
9. Early widow
10. Spiritual immaturity
11. Inexcusable mistakes
12. Demonic judgment
13. Forget when Dream
14. Non achievement in life
15. Mental problems
16. Destitute at old age
17. Menstrual problems
18. Disgraceful things in life
19. Living below expectation

# Chapter 4

# THE MYSTERY OF SACRIFICIAL LOCATIONS

For any sacrifice to take place these things need to be done. There must be:

i) An altar – this is where the spirits ascend and descend. If it is an altar of God, His Spirit comes there. If it is satanic altar there is demonic presence. A clear case in mind is when Jacob made an altar at Bethel and poured oil to invite God's presence (Genesis 28:18).

ii) Priest – The priest is the person who invokes the deity or spirit to appear through spoken words.

The presence of God on His altar brings blessings and that of Satan brings curses. For instance, when Barak wanted Balaam to curse the children of Israel, the later asked the former to build 7 altars. On each altar he was asked to sacrifice 7 animals. The full story is in Numbers 23. Just as satanic agents can build an altar to curse, so also God's altars are built to bless His children.

When Solomon wanted God's presence in his life, he went to Gideon and sacrificed 1000 burnt offering on the altar which was a distance of 4 miles from Jerusalem. The Tabernacle Moses made was located at Gideon at that time. This place was one of the most prominent places at that time.

Solomon's sacrifice invited God's presence. As said earlier any time blood is poured a spirit appears. God's spirit appeared and asked Solomon any blessing he needed and that it will be granted. Solomon asked for wisdom and it was given to him. The Bible records that Solomon was the wisest man at that time. This story could be read in 1 king 3:4-5.

Our forefathers raised altars and exchanged people's destinies for their own glory, long life, prosperity and for bravery. An altar can be located any where. Let's see examples.

**At intersections**

People are made to believe the lies of Satan to sacrifice at crossroads. This allows the witch doctors to call on demons from North, South, East and West against a person's life. We are manipulated to believe that when we break a coconut at crossroads we will be blessed. It is rather the opposite. A man was going through immigration problem in Canada. A pastor asked him to take a coconut and smash it at a crossroad and he will get his landed status. He was deported back to his home country. We need to call on God through Christ, who is our mediator and the right way. He is sitting at the right hand of God.

**Under Trees**

Another location where evil sacrifices are made is under trees. Typical examples include:

i)   lroko trees
ii)  Baobab trees
iii) Coconut trees

This principle is copied from the Bible by Satan. In Job 1:5 the Bible says job always sacrificed on behalf of his children that may be they might have sinned against God.

Sacrifices such as eggs, mashed food, are left at the based of a tree and animals blood poured on the tree's trunk. For any person to do this, a covenant has made knowingly or unknowingly with demons. We can only break it through the blood of Jesus Christ.

Pawpaw trees and mango trees are also used to do sacrifices by satanic agents in some parts of Africa.

Personal items such as clothes, umbilical cords of children are buried under those trees. Your life will be dictated by any the plant's life because they are seasonal plants.

## B. Water sacrifice

This is where we are manipulated to throw coins into a river, a sea, or a lagoon. By that method of sacrifice, you make a covenant with your spirit, soul and body to demons in that water called marine spirit. By this you are manipulated to invite marine spirit into your marriage or business. It is only through the Blood of Jesus that we can be set free from any of those sacrifices. The scripture says, "when the son sets you free you shall be free indeed."

## C. Family Shrines

Another manipulation of Satan is through family shrines. In many parts of the world people have family shrines where the family sacrifices for specific periods of the year. It could be 7 or 40 days intervals. Through those sacrifices, the entire family establishes a covenant with demonic powers. Such family names are put in a register and they begin to monitor members' movements. Even though we become born again, the covenant made by our parents are still binding for generation to generation. It is only through the power of Christ that the link could be broken.

## D. Items from persons

The enemy uses people's items to inflict them with sicknesses such skin diseases. If wicked people get hold of your clothes or underwear or anything you have ever put on your body, they can use them for sacrifice. Out of love we give our clothes to people with the aim of helping them but ends out to be perpetual bondage for us. Pray over your items before giving them out to anyone.

Our pictures can also be used by wicked men to fight our marriage, or inflict us with sickness or killed us. Even though many people claim to be born again, still they are involved in witchcraft. If a person is born into witchcraft family, he or she inherits it by birth. Just as when a person is born into the priesthood family you become a priest. The following scripture confirms that priesthood was forever, Exodus 40:14-16. God instructed Moses to anoint Aaron and his children to be priests forever. So if you come from satanic priesthood you inherit the priesthood by virtue of your birth. When this happens use the blood of Jesus to detach yourself from your background.

In a nutshell, our ancestors sacrificed to idols. They said certain words which we have no clue but they are still working in our lives for good or bad. For instance when God said to Abraham that his children will go into bondage for 400 years; it did happen. Abraham, Isaac, and Jacob did not go into bondage but their later generations. This is what happens to most of us because of what our ancestors did or said.

# Chapter 5

# Demonic Altars

**Definition of an altar:**

An altar is a place of worship, where humanity enters into a covenant with divinity. It also serves as a place where sacrifices are made to deities.

**Definition of a sacrifice:**

Sacrifice is an offering of an animal, something precious or of great value to a deity or deities for protection, vindication, appeasement; covenant or solution to problems. An altar has no power until sacrifices are made unto it. Sacrifice, therefore, is the power and the voice of an altar. Sacrifice always involves the shedding of blood or killing of something because whatever is brought to an altar must die. Satanic altars are against believers' destinies.

Satan and his agents know this principle and they always demand blood in order to operate effectively. But as believers, Christ did the sacrifice for us once and for all. So what believers need to do is to activate God's altar through giving so that God's voice will speak for us. The blood speaks for atonement for our souls (Lev 17:11).

## B. Biblical altars (Exodus 20:24-25)

Biblical altars were structures of earth on which the sacrifices were offered. They were erected in open places (Gen 22:9).

Noah was the first person to erect an altar according to scriptures (Gen 8:20). The patriarchs understood the power behind altars. We see in the Old Testament how altars were erected by Abraham (Gen 12:7; 13:4; 22:9) Isaac (Gen 26:25) and Jacob (Gen 33:20; 33:1, 3) and Moses (Exodus 17:15).

Another important thing about sacrifices is that they attract either good or bad spirits. This way depends on the person offering the sacrifice and on whose altar. For our explanation and understanding let's read what God told Abraham.

And built an altar unto the Lord, and took of every clean, beast, and of every clean fowl and offered burnt offering on the altar … and day and night shall not cease. (Gen 8:20-22)

After a sacrifice is offered a spirit appears and begins to make pronouncements and covenants. As stated earlier, blood has voice and, therefore, speaks. So as an altar is empowered through the sacrifice, God appeared and promised never to use water to destroy living things or curse the ground again.

So anytime we sacrifice on either God's altar or Satanic altar a voice comes and work on our behalf. Another person who understood the principle of sacrifice was Abraham. In Gen 15:1-19 God demanded sacrifice from Abraham that he could enter into a covenant relationship with him.

> And when the sun was going down a deep sleep fell on Abram; and lo, a horror of great darkness fell on him. And he said unto Abram, know of a surety that thy seed….. In the same day the Lord made a covenant with Abraham, saying 'unto thy seed have I given this land from the river of Egypt into the great river, the river Euphrates (Gen 15:12-18).

In this covenant, God appeared after the sacrifice and promises Abraham the following:

- Descendants to be like the stars in the sky or grain of sand on the seashore. In order words, God promised to bless him beyond measure or his generation. Again, we learn that Abraham's faith in the Lord made him right with God. If we are believers trust in the Lord, have confidence in him and a right relationship based on inner heartfelt confidence that God is who He says He and will never disappoint or fail us.

- That Abrahams descendants will be strangers in a foreign land where they will be oppressed as slaves for 400 years.

- That Abrahams descendant after the oppression will be delivered miraculously. God did exactly what he said when He took them out of slavery after 430 years through Moses.

- The Israelites left Egypt with great wealth as God promised.

Again, we learn that God made a covenant with Abraham so many years earlier of what will happen to his descendants and everything happened as God said. In the same way our great grandparents signed contracts with demonic altars or priests and today we are paying for the price. Some of the contracts our parents signed were in search of solutions to their problems. Another important sacrifice is that of King Solomon:

> And Solomon went up thither to the brazen altar before the Lord which was at the tabernacle of the congregation and offered a thousand burnt offerings upon it in that night did God appeared unto Solomon… neither shall there any after thee have the like. (2 Chronicle 1:6-12).

Why did Solomon give so much sacrifice? Solomon knew that sacrifice activates spiritual laws into motion. He needed God to do something extraordinary in his kingdom and in his life. After the sacrifice, God appeared to him and asked what he wanted. Solomon said, he needed wisdom to rule Israel. God granted his request.

Bible scholars tell us that, that was the Tabernacle Moses had built centuries earlier as God's home on Earth. It was about 500 years later that Solomon replaced the Tabernacle with the Temple which became a central place of Israel's worship. God also filled the Temple with His glory as He did to the Tabernacle in the days of Moses (2 Chronicle 5:13-14).

Anytime Israel turned from God, the glory and the presence of the Lord departed from the Temple. God's departure, made it possible for Israel's enemies to destroy it by invading enemies. When the presence of the Lord leaves us, the enemy is able to attack our lives at will.

It is believed by Biblical scholars that, the Temple was rebuilt 515 BC. God's glory returned to it even in greater dimension. Christ taught in this second Tabernacle. When Christ was crucified, buried and raised, God's glory again departed because the Tabernacle didn't need any physical building to dwell in... God's Temple now is in the body of believers. So keep your body clean from sin for God's spirit to dwell there.

Looking at Solomon's answer to God's question of what he needed. He asked for wisdom. Solomon knew that wisdom is the ability to make good decisions based on proper discernment and judgment. In order words, Solomon asked for practical know how necessary for handling everyday matters including wealth. Solomon applied the wisdom God gave him to build the Temple his father had plan and to put Israel on a firm economic footing.

Solomon realized that wisdom is important to his kingship than riches. He later confirms this to us when he said "wisdom is more precious than rubies, nothing you desire can compare with it" (Prov. 3:15). Even though

Solomon put his nation before his own needs, God added wealth, riches and honor to him. This means that when we put God first, everything we really need will be given to us as well. What it means again is that when we put God first, the, wisdom He gives will enable us to hake richly rewarding lives.

## Effects of Parental Sins

The scripture clearly tells us that there are consequences to pay for the evil that our ancestors did. Let's read this scripture:

Our fathers have sinned and are not; and we have born their iniquities. Servants have ruled over us... For this our heart is faint, for these things our eyes are din (Lam 5:7-17).

From this passage we see consequences we go through as a result of what our parents did in the past without our knowledge or consent.

## 1. Servants Rule Over

People we are suppose to rule now rule over us. God said we should be fruitful which, was the first blessing God pronounced on humanity. Every area of our lives should be fruitful. We don't see that fruitfulness in our lives. Those who don't deserve to be our masters are now telling us what to do. Today sicknesses, poverty, non-achievement, barrenness of believers, disagrce and shame have become our masters.

## 2. We seek deliverance prayers with no results.

The hand of the Lord is not short nor his ears deaf that he does not hear but because of sins of our parents and ours we receive no answers to our prayers.

## 3. Our daily living through struggles.

We make so much effort working two or three jobs with little or no results. We are able to produce and feed our families while others have built factories, big businesses. All those could be traced back to family backgrounds.

## 4. Immorality among the Youth

Young people below majority age group are forced into prostitution because of circumstances beyond their control. Peoples' lives are shortened because they have contracted all manner of venereal diseases such as HIV or gonorrhea. Many young people are turned to prostitution against their consciences. This is because our fathers have sinned and the enemy has used it as a stepping stone to destroy lives of innocent people.

## 5. Noble hands are tied up

We see our youth with much potential roaming the streets our cities jobless their destinies have been repacked. They resort to arm robbery, fraud, drug peddling and all manner of evil devices. Why? The sins of our fathers have affected their potentials.

## 6. No respect for The Elderly

Men of questionable characters are now in charge of affairs of our society. Gray hair is no longer considered a mark of old age and respect. What has gone wrong?

## 7. The dilemma of our youths

Our youths especially blacks fills the prisons of the western world. There are so many questions bothering the minds of these youths. They ask themselves "why me?" They look for solutions to their problems. Who is to take the blame for these numerous problems confronting the youth?

## 8. Our children in slavery

Most children roam the streets to sell wares in the big cities of third world countries. Some drop out of school to sell goods, while their age groups are in schools pursuing careers. Many people from third world countries are important personalities but are now slavery. Why? Our fathers' sins are the reasons.

## 9.  Elders have left their Responsibilities

The Elders who are supposed to stay in our villages, towns, and cities have left in pursuit of wealth. The elders who are supposed to stay and impart knowledge to the youth, discipline and core family values to the youth, are no where to be seen. Many valuable cultures, values and, discipline are no longer observed. Why? Our fathers have sinned.

## 10. No more joy

We cry daily because our seeds die in the ground and harvests have continuously eluded us. The joy of the Lord is our strength. Why are we not experiencing that joy as believers? What is the reason for our fears? Our fathers have sin.

## 11. Our dancing Turns into Mourning

Anytime we expect joy we see sorrows. We marry with the aim of enjoying our marriage but turns out to be divorce. We expect fruitfulness but in our marriages we see barrenness. Early in the morning we might feel very sorrowful because we are going through the same results in our efforts. We question ourselves where the God that we serve is. Has God abandoned us? No. Our Fathers have sinned.

## 12. Our crown has fallen

**The** honor and glory God gave us have been taken from us. Even though we are believers still we don't see fruitfulness in our lives as God said to us in His Word. What has stopped the blessing of the Lord into our lives. Why? Our fathers have sinned and we are reaping the consequences.

## 13. Our Hearts faint

Many believers are confused about life. We no longer know which way to turn to. Others are running to Satan and his agents thereby complicating issues. We are fed up with life because history is repeating itself in a negative way. Truly our hearts faint because our efforts produce no tangible results but tears and sorrows.

## 14. Our Eyes are dim

Spiritually, we cannot see far. We cannot discern. We cannot plan far and succeed. Why is that so? Our parents have sinned. They are no more there but we bear the consequences.

# Chapter 6

# The consequences of idol worship

A.    Satan knows the mystery and power behind blood on an altar. He, therefore, manipulated our forefathers to build altars to sacrifice on them. By so doing, he and his agents lay hold on members of a family and continue their wicked activities. Those sacrifices have become voices that fight us at the point of success.

The altars were used as places of worship and places covenants were made and sealed with blood from those sacrifices. These sacrifices become pattern in the family, repeatition of family negative history.

Even though we are believers, many troubles we go through are a continuation of what had been in existence before us. Paul tells us in Rom 5:18 that through one man's offence sin came into the world. So what our ancestors did have affected us.

Nobody who is a believer or a Jew today knows patriarch Abraham, but his faith has made us partakers and heirs of his blessings "every house is built by some man" the Bible states in Heb 3:4. Therefore, what we are going through is the same spirit that fought our parents is also fighting us. For instance, our fathers might set a limit to the progress of family members. When you reach that limit they come in and remind you not ignore that information. For a better understanding of these evil family patterns, examine what goes on in your life and in the family of both mom and dad.

## B. Biblical Illustration

God saw Abraham's background and still called him at age 75. He was an idol worshipper married to Sarah. They were serving the Lord faithful. Whoever thought they will have the problem of child bearing. There was barrenness in the family blood line. During my visit to Israel in 2012 I learned that Abraham did not only worship an idol but had a shop to sell idols to customers. It is no surprise the following evil pattern happened in the family blood line.

a. Sarah, Abraham's wife was barren

b. Rebecca, Isaac's wife was barren

c. Rachael, Jacob's wife was barren

C. Let's look at another important evil pattern that worked through Abraham's bloodline.

   1. Ishmael was the first born of Abraham. Ishmael lost his birth right to Isaac, his younger brother.

   2. Esau was the first son of Isaac. Isaac lost his birth right to Jacob his younger brother.

   3. Ruben was the first son of Jacob. Ruben lost his birth right to Joseph

   4. Manasseh was the first son of Joseph. Manasseh lost his birth right to his younger brother, Ephraim.

   From those biblical illustrations we could see that even though we are believers we experience similar patterns in our families. Some families experience divorce among the females at a certain age. Others after birth to a male or female child. Others have stable marriage but live in abject poverty. Others marry but hardly give birth to children. Others reach a certain age in life and are inflicted with a sickness or die prematurely.

   In all these mysteries and family evil patterns fighting us today, were raised by our ancestors but they still work against us. Our parents made covenants at strange and demonic altars and we now reap the results. Another important point is that those evil patterns occur either from mom's or dad's lineage.

The only way to stop evil and wicked pattern is to set up a new altar with a sacrifice and silence them through prayers. We also need to do research because in some cases there is no body alive to give us details of what took place in our family. We, therefore, have to turn to the Holy Spirit, who is all-knowing for help.

In our research we need to ask these questions:

1. Why did my father/ mother stopped where she/ stopped?

2. Why did my uncles, Aunties stopped where they stopped.

3. Why is it that I am also going through the poverty, divorce, barrenness, non-achievements, backwardness, mental problem, late marriage, etc.

If what we are going through was started by somebody then somebody can stop it as well. There is a popular saying that, "The lion you refuse to kill today will kill you tomorrow." This means the issue we refuse to confront today will surface sometime later. So it is important to research and know the source of problems in order to confront them. We cannot confront what we don't know.

**Nicely Packaged but Empty**

There was a man born to be great and to be a judge in Israel. He was born into a family that worshipped idols. He neither chose his place of birth nor his parents. I believe God did that on purpose. Poverty and untold suffering was the order of the day for this man.

This man called Gideon could not do anything about the situation because he did not know what was wrong. He joined the toiling of the family even though he was packed by God to be a ruler. His life did not change until he had an encounter with the angel of the Lord to tell him what to do. Till we seek the help of the Holy Spirit to reveal to us what to do about our situation, we will remain stagnant in life. As believers, we ask the same question Gideon asked "If God is with me why going through all these sufferings". Others asked, "Has God forsaken us? Where are His promises for His children? People ask those questions because there are no physical evidence accompanying our deliverance, prayers, fasting and confession of God promises. In other words, our practical experiences are contrary to God's promises, our prayer requests, and prophecies we might have received from men of God.

Our fathers have sinned. They are no more but we bear the consequence. Now Gideon is instructed by the Lord to do something to end the suffering in his family and the entire nation. God revealed the source of his poverty, suffering, struggling without evidence, laboring without reward. Gideon was instructed to do the following:

1.   Destroy the altar of Baal in the family house
2.   Build a new altar in its place
3.   Offer burn offering on the new altar

These three instructions were the issues to deal with. They have stopped Gideon in the same spot for a long time. Gideon is instructed to cut the link between the past and the present. Issues in the past that have stopped him in the same spot. Through deliverance, Gideon will be able to reach his destiny. The old altar's assignment was to keep Gideon where it kept his family. By destroying our past we may be able to reach the level God designed us to be.

Finally, Gideon is asked to build a new altar and sacrifice on it. It is the voice of the new sacrifice that will speak. As we also sacrifice after going through deliverance, we receive favor. The new altar and sacrifices, which is the Blood of Jesus, disarms those demonic powers and attracts the Holy Spirit. From

Gideon's example, we see that fasting, deliverance, and prayers are good but without building a new altar and sacrificing on it, there will be little result for our efforts.

Sacrifice attracts the presence of spirits and activates all spiritual laws into motion to intervene in a man's affairs (Isa 49:24-26). God contends with those who contend with our destiny. The only way God fights our enemies and to drink their own blood is through our sacrifice. In modern terminology we will say our giving

Our fathers empowered demonic altars to operate in the family through their sacrifices. Our sacrifices (giving) on God's altar activates the Blood of Jesus to stop any spirit designed to work against us. Another thing worthy of note is Gideon's obedience. Every instruction giving him was obeyed to the letter.

The enemy planned to attack but Gideon had done something new God was happy about. They did not know that their legal ground, that is the old altar has been destroyed. When God came into the life of Gideon the evil pattern changed. He got help from:

- People from his village and tribe.
- Families of Elders who sought to kill him before. Two most important people God brought to help Gideon as a result of his sacrifice where

a. Advertisers

Advertisers: Our advertisers will do the following for us;

- Introduce us to destiny helpers
- Projects our person and potentials
- The old altar that gives wrong information about us would begin to give good information about us.
- Identify us with garment of shame and disgrace
- Will speak in our favor at right place, as John the Baptist did by introducing Jesus Christ of Nazareth (Math 3:13-17)

b. Helpers:

- More helpers (e.g. Gideon had 32.000 men) to go to war with him
- Ready to take instructions from him
- From least to most important were around him
- From poor family to the richest family in Manasseh
- Became a judge without campaigning for the position

We can become the Gideon of our family. The answer and solution our family has been waiting and crying for over the years. We have become born again for this purpose. Let's through prayers change the evil occurrences in our families. Let's do something to stop the poverty, lack, non-achievement, barrenness, miscarriages etc. in our lives.

For a change to take place, it must cost us something valuable. Let's change position like Gideon who took his name out of the family's circle of evil pattern and non-achievement. The following reasons made Gideon Successful after building a new altar with a valuable sacrifice.

1. God's spirit came on him to do exploits
2. His helpers and advertisers heard his voice and obeyed.
3. The grace to accomplish much with little (300 people)
4. He defeated his enemies no matter how many they are
5. He stepped into the next level of his life to fulfill his destiny
6. He ruled what once ruled him
7. He changed that of his status including his family
8. He brought an end to poverty to himself and family
9. He was in change of the affairs of the family

We can become the Gideon of our individual families, the answer and solution our families have been awaiting and crying for all those years. Build a new altar and give a valuable sacrifice on it for a change to take place.

# Chapter 7

# The Mystery of Evil Sacrifices

## A. Animals

Satan copies whatever is in the word of God. When Adam and Eve did sin God killed an animal in order to atone for their sin. They realized their nakedness after they had sinned. This is recorded in Gen 3:21.

Even though many people are Christians but our backgrounds show that our parents did animal sacrifices to idols. Blood attracts spirits. The highest blood always dominates. This is why Abel's sacrifice dominated that of Cain who brought only sacrifice of farm produce. This could not attract the spirit of God. Abel understood the meaning of sacrifice as killing something in order to save another. Abel also understood that sacrifice as a means of making an appeal to a deity in order to establish a relation with that deity, God or gods. Cain misunderstood sacrificed and so his sacrifice was not accepted. His understanding of the principle came too late. He experimented on his brother which was too late and wrong. We should always be led by the Holy Spirit to do things at the right time.

## B. Incisions

Many people from many parts of the world receive incision on their belly, cheek, forehead or wrist. Witchdoctors use those means to draw blood from the human body. They manipulate our parents that it is a means of protection or solution to our problems. It is quite the opposite.

Anytime we do incisions we are under a curse because these agents of Satan recite words over us which we do not understand. This is called witchcraft manipulation. Through any of these incisions, a covenant is established. Your own blood has been used to seal the covenant knowingly or unknowingly. A covenant of blood is a strong bond that binds you to God, spirits or evil powers. In the scriptures God made a covenant with Abraham, blood was used to seal it God asked Abraham to circumcise including his household. God still honors that sacrifice for many years now.

Many of us are going through many problems financially and in our marriages because of evil covenants our parents performed ignorantly. Transference of spirits took place. We exchanged something for something else. Tattoos are the modern form of incisions. The blood of Jesus is the only blood that can nullify any other blood covenant. Christ came to sacrifice the highest blood to redeem us.

## C. Human Sacrifice

Human sacrifice is when somebody kills a human being to obtain his blood for praying purposes. Demons and evil forces respond when a family member kills a person and the blood touches the ground or an object the blood cries out for vengeance. This is why the innocent blood of Abel cried for revenge and God appeared to question Cain about the whereabouts of Abel. The scripture says "for the life of the flesh is I the blood" (Lev 11:7).

There is an automatic curse on any family that sheds innocent blood. The sacrifice has given mandate to evil spirits to frustrates your life, cause stagnation and cause backwardness to you and your generations to the third and fourth.

## D. Fowls Sacrifice

Another witchcraft manipulation is that of Sacrifice we make using fowls such as chicken, pigeon or doves. Whatever means to kill any fowl for sacrifices to an altar or anything is witchcraft manipulation. Whatever means use the kill does not matter. The fact is you have established a blood covenant between you and the spirit addressed, and the land or ground. When this is done the land becomes dedicated to the spirits or spirit that the covenant is made.

The blood offered is not made to God Almighty but to a demon or demons. The performing who offered the fowl's life has now been bound to a demon.

In Gen 15:9-10 God made a covenant with Abraham. Abraham was asked to bring a bird and other animals. Five animals in total. The number five stand for grace. After this sacrifice Abraham received God's grace. A blood covenant was made between Abraham and God. God promised to give him a child. This happened in the person of Isaac. As a confirmation of this prophecy God added that Abraham's descendants shall be strangers in a foreign land for about 400 years. This prophecy was fulfilled as Stephen confirms in Act 7:6-8. Covenants are real and you cannot easily break them except through deliverance and the use of the Blood of Jesus which is higher than any other blood.

### E. Grave yards sacrifice

Another witchcraft manipulation in some parts of the world is to deceive many people to bury hair, a picture, clothing, finger nails, or any item from our body at any burial ground. It is a way of holding somebody's destiny. These things are done to invite the spirit of death into the family. Many people face problems in marriages, finances, as a result of what might have been sacrificed or buried at grave yards. Don't accept this manipulation any longer from Satan and his agents because you are now born again.

## Money Sacrifice

This kind of sacrifice is another manipulation of witchcraft spirit. The enemy leaves us with intention of making us rich but turns out to be the opposite. The Bible states that it is the blessing of the Lord that makes us rich.

People are deceived to give money to evil altars, shrines or throw money into a river or at certain junctions. We are trapped into financial hardships because of ignorance. The scripture says "it is the blessing of the Lord that makes us rich and adds no sorrow it". The devil is able to make us to believe him because he knows that people love money. The scripture rightly says in part that, "For the love of money is a root of all kinds of evil" (1 Timothy 6:10).

## Menstrual Blood sacrifice

This is when a woman donates her menstrual pad to satanic altar for the purpose of getting pregnancy.

We must remember that life is in the blood as Leviticus 11:7 declares. Therefore, to give your menstrual pad to somebody is another way of given your blood to your enemy. It looks ridiculous when a pastor asks a lady looking for the fruit of the womb to bring her menstrual pad to pray over in order to let the woman get pregnant. This is witchcraft manipulation. This is not recorded in the scriptures. Don't do it next time.

# Chapter 8

# The Mystery of Hearing from God

From the time of Moses, God started speaking to humankind through various means. He spoke through the prophets and has continued to speak to his children today. This is because He is the same yesterday, today, and forever. Let's look at some of the ways our Father speaks to us as his children.

## A. Through His Word (2 Timothy 3:16)

One of the ways God speaks to believers today is through the Bible. God used audible voice and spoke to Moses several times (Exodus 19:19-21). Also God used angels to speak to us as recorded in Heb 2:2. This scripture refers to the instructions given by angels such as Lot's wife as recorded in Gen 19:17-26 and that of Sampson birth in Judges 13:5.

We need to be very careful because Satan has his demonic angels who bring messages through people. Whatever God does Satan also copies it. There are records in the scriptures how God spoke through the prophets of Old (Heb 1:1). The Holy Spirit indwelt he dwells in men today. Whatever was written down in the scriptures are for instructions from God through those prophets.

## B. The Apostles

God also spoke to humankind through the Apostles as recorded in Acts 1:2 which reads, "until the day in which he was taken up, after that he through the Holy Ghost had given commandments unto the Apostles who He had chosen. This Holy Spirit refers to God's own spirit speaking to the Twelve Apostles. He had Christ spirit hence Christ spoke to them we also as believers have Christ Spirit and He speaks to us depending on our relationship with God.

## C. Dreams

Another means God spoke to people of old as well as present is through dreams.

There are 14 important dreamers recorded in the scriptures. They include:

- **Abimelech (Genesis 20:3,6)**

"But God came to Abimelech in a dream by night, and said to him," "indeed you are a dead man because of the woman you have taken, for she is a man's wife."

- **Jacob (Genesis 28:12)**

"Then he dreamed and behold a ladder was set up on the earth, and its top reach up to heaven, and there the angels of God were ascending and descending on it."

- **Laban (Genesis 31:24)**

But God had come to Laban, the Syrian, in a dream by night, and said to him, "Be careful that you speak to Jacob neither good nor bad".

- **Joseph (Gen 37:5-10)**

"Now Joseph had a dream, and he told it to his brothers; and they hated him even more. So he said to them, "Please hear this dream which I have dreamed: "There we were, binding sheaves in the field. Then behold, my sheaf arose and also stood upright; and indeed your sheaves stood all around and bowed down to my sheaf." And his brothers said to him, "Shall you indeed reign over us? Or shall you indeed have dominion over us?" So they hated him even more for his dreams and for his words. Then he dreamed still another dream and told it to his brothers, and said,

"Look, I have dreamed another dream. And this time, the sun, the moon, and the eleven stars bowed down to me." So he told it to his father and his brothers; and his father rebuked him and said to him, "what is this dream that you have dreamed? Shall your mother and I and your brothers indeed come to bow down to the earth before you?"

- **The Chief Butler (Gen 40:9-15)**

Then the chief butler told his dream to Joseph, and said to him, "Behold, in my dream a vine was before me, "and in the vine were three branches; it was as though it budded, its blossoms shot forth, and its clusters brought forth ripe grapes. "Then Pharaoh's cup was in my hand; and I took the grapes and pressed them into Pharaoh's cup, and placed the cup in Pharaoh's hand." And Joseph said to him "This is the interpretation of it: The three branches are three days. "Now within three days Pharaoh will lift up your head and restore you to your place, and you will put Pharaoh's cup in his hand according to the former manner, when you were his butler. "But remember me when it is well with you, and please show kindness to me; make mention of me to Pharaoh, and get me out of this house. "For indeed I was stolen away from the land of the Hebrews; and also I have done nothing here that they should put me into the dungeon."

- **The chief baker (Gen 40:16-23)**

When the chief baker saw that the interpretation was good, he said to Joseph, "I also saw in my dream, and there were three white baskets on my head. "In the uppermost basket were all kinds of baked goods for Pharaoh, and the birds ate them out of the basket on my head." So Joseph answered and said, "This is the interpretation of it: The three baskets are three days. "Within three days Pharaoh will lift off your head from you and hang you on a tree; and the birds will eat your flesh from you."

Now it came to pass on the third day, which was Pharaoh's birthday that he made a feast for all his servants; and he lifted up the head of the chief butler and of the chief baker among his servants. Then he restored the chief butler to his butlership again, and he placed the cup in Pharaoh's hand. But he hanged the chief baker, as Joseph had interpreted to them. Yet the chief butler did not remember Joseph, but forgot him.

- **Pharaoh (Gen 41:1-3)**

Then it came to pass, at the end of two full years, that Pharaoh had a dream; and behold, he stood by the river. Suddenly there came up out of the river seven cows, fine looking and fat; and they fed in the meadow. Then behold, seven other cows came up after them out of the river, ugly and gaunt, and stood by the other cows on the bank of the river.

- **A Moabite (Judges 7:13-15)**

And when Gideon had come, there was a man telling a dream to his companion. He said, "I have had a dream: to my surprise, a loaf of barley bread tumbled into the camp of Midian; it came to a tent and struck it so that it fell and overturned, and the tent collapsed." Then his companion answered and said, "This is nothing else but the sword of Gideon the son of Joshua, a man of Israel! Into his hand God has delivered Midian and the whole camp." And so it was, when Gideon heard the telling of the dream and its interpretation, that he worshipped. He returned to the camp of Israel, and said, "Arise, for the LORD has delivered the camp of Median into your hand."

- **King Solomon**

At Gibeon, the Lord appeared to Solomon in a dream by night and said, "Ask! What shall I give you?" And Solomon said:

You have shown great mercy to your servant David my father, because he walked before you in truth, in righteousness, and in uprightness of heart with You; You have continued this great kindness for him, and You have given him a son to sit on his throne, as it is this day. Now, O Lord my God, You have made Your servant king instead of my father David, but I am a little child; I do not know how to go out or come in. "And Your servant is in the midst of Your people whom You have chosen, a great people, too numerous to be numbered or counted. "Therefore give your servant an understanding heart to judge Your people, that I may discern between good and evil. For who is able to judge this great people of yours?"

The speech pleased the Lord, that Solomon had asked this thing. Then God said to him: "Because you have asked this thing, and have not asked long life for yourself, nor have asked riches for yourself, nor have asked the life of your enemies, but have asked for yourself understanding to discern justice, behold, I have done according to your words; see, I have given you a wise and understanding heart, so that there has not been anyone like you before you, nor shall any like you arise after you. "And I have also given you what you have not asked: both riches and honor, so that there shall not be anyone like you among the kings all your days. "So if you walk in My ways, to keep My statutes and My commandments, as your father David walked, then I will lengthen your days." (1 King 3:5-15)

Then Solomon awoke; and indeed it had been a dream. And he came to Jerusalem and stood before the ark of the covenant of the Lord, offered up burnt offerings, offered peace offerings, and made a feast for all his servants.

- **Nebuchadnezzar (Daniel 2:7)**

They answered again and said, "Let the king tell his servants the dream, and we will give its interpretation."

This was a situation when King Nebuchadnezzar had a dream that he did not understand and his spirit was so disturbed that he needed some explanation. God gave the interpretation to Daniel so as to save Daniel and his friends who were in prison and to demonstrate that God answers prayers. Again, God was demonstrating to the king that He was greater than the wise men and to make it clear that God is the author of prophecies.

- **Joseph (Mathew 1:20)**

But while he though about these things, behold, an angel of the Lord appeared to him in a dream, saying, "Joseph, son of David, do not be afraid to take to you Mary your wife, for that which is conceived in her is of the Holy Spirit.

Through a dream God spoke to Joseph who was Mary's fiancée. Joseph was planning to divorce many secretly because she was found pregnant when the wedding had not taken place. God sent the Angel Gabriel to Joseph not to divorce Mary because she was conceived of the Holy Spirit (Mathew 1:20). The Lord spoke to Joseph at three other times as Matthew records in Mathew1:24; 2:13, 19. There are several instances in both Old and New

Testaments when God spoke to His children through dreams as seen in those scriptures we have just examined.

## • Daniel 2:1-3

We have another good example found in Dan 2:1-3 where King Nebuchadnezzar saw an image. He was very troubled because he did not understand what it meant. The King's magicians could not interpret it either until Daniel was called in to interpret the meaning of it (Dan 2:36-45). Through the assistance of the Holy Spirit, Daniel gave interpretation to the dream that King Nebuchadnezzar had that troubled his spirit.

Not only did Daniel interpret the King's dream but was able to tell the king what he saw in his dream. He told the King that he saw a great image of different materials:

- The head of gold: This symbolized the first of five kingdoms
- The beast and arms of silver: The Medo–Persian Kingdom that succeeded Babylon
- The belly and thighs of brass: This represents Grecian Empire under Alexander the Great
- The legs of iron: This symbolized the Old Roman Empire
- The feet and toes of iron and clay: Represent the future Roman Empire.

Everything happened as Daniel interpreted by Daniel according to historical facts.

- **The 3 Wise Men**

  "Then being divinely warned in a dream that they should not return to Herod, they departed from their own country another way" (Matthew 2:12)

  This was when the wise men came looking for the baby Jesus after he was born in Bethlehem. But spoke to them in a dream not to go back to Herod because he the intention to destroy Jesus. The blood of Jesus covers your children as a child of God.

- **Pilates Wife**

  "While he was sitting on the judgment seat, his wife sent for him, saying, 'have nothing to do with that Man for I have suffered many things in a dream because of Him" (Matthew 27:19)

### Inspiration

God also spoke to people in both the past and present through inspiration. The Lord used 40 authors to write the 66 books of the Bible. Today God uses inspiration to speak to the body of Christ. Through inspiration men wrote down what God instructed them to write to his followers. God continue to do the same through the preaching of the Word of God. Many lives are transformed through messages given by God to men and women of God.

**Visions**

God also speaks to us through visions. God uses visions to speak to his church and individuals both in the past and today. Paul had a vision of our Lord Jesus Christ on his way to Damascus to harass believers (Acts 9:3-7). In the same book of Acts 10, it is recorded how Cornelius received vision from the Lord.

Another vision recorded is found in Gen 15:1 when the Lord assured Abraham not to be afraid because God was with him. There are several records of men who saw visions both in the Old and New Testaments. In the Old Testament, the following men had visions from the Lord: Jacob (Gen 46:2), Samuel (1 Sam 3:1,15) and Isaiah (Isaiah 1:1). In the New Testament, the following men also received visions:

- Peter (Acts 16:19)
- Ananias (Acts 9:9-12)
- Apostle Paul (Acts 16:9-10)

If you seek him, you will find Him to speak to you.

## Inaudible (Small) Voice

Another means the Lord speaks to His children is through a small inaudible or loud audible voice. In 1 King 19:12-15 a small voice spoke to the Prophet Elijah when he was running away from Jezebel. God spoke to him in a small voice, "And after the earthquake a fire, but the Lord was not in the fire and after the fire, a small voice," (v12).

This is a lesson to us that those who believe that loud, boisterous and highly demonstrative worship is a mark of power from God while that of quietness and gentle is a sign of lack of the spirit. In some occasions, God was revealed in mighty thundering as seen in Rev 10:3-4 and Exodus 20:18. Other examples recorded in the Bible include Samuel when God called him three times but he did not know who was calling. Paul on his way to Damascus in Acts 9:4-5 and a voice that came to Moses at the burning bush in (Exodus.3:16).

A good example of an audible voice as recorded in the Bible is found in Mathew 17:5-6. The voice that Peter, James and John heard was a clear evidence of God's presence. In this passage Moses and Elijah were sent to confirm Christ as the Messiah, the sole authority from God and the Mediator between God and man.

**Tongues**

Another means God uses to speak to the church is through speaking in Tongues. In 1 Corinthians 12:4-11 Paul talks about speaking in Tongues. To speak in tongues means the ability to speak in legitimate tongues or language that the recipient of the gift has never learned. The speaker does not understand what he or she says. This tongue is a sign for believers that, those that have this gift of speaking in tongues are born again and are spirit-filled. This is a kind of tongues speaking Paul advises to use in our private prayer time.

The second type of Tongues Paul mentions is the Tongues God uses to speak to the church as a whole to edify the congregation. This kind of Tongues speaking is a mystery because the speaker prays about matters he or she knows not. Also by praying in tongues, selfishness in our prayers is eliminated. This kind of Tongues praying brings us in agreement with the Holy Spirit to intercede for people who need our prayers.

Through these various means, God still speaks to his children who have closed relationship with Him.

# Chapter 9

# Your Daily Manna

## A. Prayers for Healing and Health

These prayers need to be prayed three times daily. Preferably in the morning, afternoon and evening. By praying these prayers daily your life will be like a tree planted by the riverside.

1. Forgive me Lord for allowing any unforgiveness, sin, pride, or rebellion to open the door to any sickness or infirmity. I renounce these things in the name of Jesus Christ of Nazareth.

2. I cast out any spirit of infirmity that came into my life through witchcraft spirit in the name of Jesus.

3. Give me a sound heart which is the life of my flesh. Remove from my heart any evil or sinful attitude in the name of Jesus Christ of Nazareth.

4.  I rebuke any sickness that would come to eat up my flesh including cancer in the name of Jesus (Ps 27:2) Christ

5.  Let not evil disease cleave to my body (Ps 41:8)

6.  I break all curses of sickness and diseases and I command all hereditary spirits of sickness to come out of my body in the name of Jesus Christ (Gal 3:13)

7.  I break all curses of premature death and destruction in the never of Jesus Christ

8.  Lord blesses my bread and water and takes sickness away from me. (Exodus 23:25) in Jesus' name.

9.  I command every organ in my body to function the way God intended (Psalm 139:14)

10. Let any tumor or evil growth, in my body melt at the presence at the Holy Spirit (Psalm 95:5)

11. I pray for my arteries and blood vessels to be opened and my circulatory system to function properly in the name of Jesus Christ of Nazareth.

12. My flesh shall be fresher than that of a child and I will return to the days of my youth (Job 33:25) in the name of Jesus Christ.

13. I pray for my immune system to be strengthened in the name of Jesus Christ (Ps 119:28)

14. Lord renew my youth like the eagle's (Ps 103:5)

15. I will live and not die and I will proclaim the name of the Lord (Ps 118: 17)

16. Heal me oh Lord and I shall be healed (Jer 17:14).

17. I release the fire of God to burn out any sickness or disease that would operate in my body in the name of Jesus.

18. No sickness or plague comes near my dwelling (Ps 91:10)

19. I command every germ, or sickness that touches my body to die in the name of Jesus.

20. Every plague is stopped. when it comes near me through the atonement blood of Jesus Christ (Num 16:50)

21. I am fearfully and wonderfully made. Lord, let my body function in a wonderful way you intended it to function (Ps 139:14) in Jesus' name.

22. I am healed by the 39 stripes of Jesus Christ (Isa 53:5)

23. Jesus carried my sickness and infirmities (Math 8:17)

24. I speak healing and strength to my bones, muscles, joints organs, head, eyes, throat, gland, blood, marrow, lungs, kidneys, liver spleen, spine, pancreas, bladder, ears, nose, sinuses mouth tongue and feet in the name of Jesus.

25. I loose myself from any weakened immune system that is rooted in a broken spirit, or broken heart and I command these spirits to come out in the name of Jesus Christ.

### B. Prayers for financial release (Deut 8:18)

Read Deut 8:18 before you declare these prayer.

By praying these prayers daily the favor of the Lord will be released in your finances.

1. I break all curses of poverty, lack, debt, stagnation, and failure in the name of Jesus

2. I seek first the kingdom of God and his righteousness and all things are added unto me (Math 6:33)

3. I cast out all spirits of the caner worm, palmer worm caterpillar and locust that will eat up my blessings in Jesus name (Joel 2:25)

4. You are Jehovah-Jireh, my provider (Gen 22:14) Provide all my needs this day in Jesus name

5. You are El Shaddai, the God of more than enough provide enough of all my needs

6. The blessing of the Lord upon my life makes me nice I am therefore, bless coming in and blessed going out

7. Jesus became poor that through His poverty I might be rich (2 Cor 8:9)

8.  Through your favor I will be a prosperous person (Gen 39:2)

9.  Lord release the weak of the wicked in to my hands (Prov 13:22)

10. I give and it is given back to me in good measure pressed down, shaken together, and running over (Luke 6:38)

11. Lord open the floodgates of heaven over my life, and I receive more than I have enough room to receives (Matt 3:10)

12. Let every hole in my bag (pocket) be closed in the name of Jesus Christ (Haggai 1:6)

13. Rebuke the devourer for my sake (Matt 3:11)

14. Let your showers of blessing come upon my life (Ezek 34:26)

15. Lead me into a land flowing with milk and honey (Exo 3:8)

16. Let me have riches and honor, in abundance (2 Chron 18:1)

17. I receive riches and honor, durable riches and righteousness (Prov 8:18)

18. I refuse to allow the angel of blessing to depart without blessing me (Gen 2:6)

19. Arrows of financial embarrassment backfire now in Jesus name

20. Any human personality that steals my finance, vomit them now by thunder in Jesus name

21. Let every evil pit and pot that keeps my money vomit them and receive destruction in Jesus name

22. Let every witchcraft manipulation against my financial breakthroughs be scattered by fire now in Jesus name.

23. Father in Heaven, release upon me this day your power to get wealth

24. Lord let the power of financial dominion begin to manifest in my life in Jesus name

25. Through your favor I will be prosperous

26. Lord teach me to profit and lead me in the way

27. I should go

28. Lord lead me into a land without scarcity and lack but a land flowing with milk and honey in Jesus name.

## C. Warfare Prayers for Victory

1. Lord teach my hands to wage war and my fingers to fight (Ps 144:1)

2. The weapons of my warfare are not carnal but mighty through you to the pulling down of strongholds (2 Cor 10:4)

3. Lord thunder upon the enemy, release your voice, hail stones and coal of fire against them (Ps 18:14)

4. You have given me the necks of my enemies, and I will destroy them in the name of Jesus (Ps 18:10)

5. I tread upon serpents and scorpions and over all the powers of the enemy and nothing shall by any means hurt me (Luke 10:19)

6. Lord lift up a standard against any flood the enemy would try to bring into my life (Isa 59:19)

7. I bind and rebuke any demon that would try to block my way in the name of Jesus (Math 8:28)

8. I break off any fellowship with devils through sin, the flesh, or sacrifice, in the name of Jesus Christ of Nazareth (1 Cor 10:20)

9. Lord expose any human devils in my life in the name of Jesus (John 6:70)

10. Lord expose any children of the devil that would try to come into the church of God in Jesus name (Acts 13:10)

11. I nullify the power of any sacrifice made to devils in my city, region, or country in the name of Jesus (Lev 17:17)

12. Lord guide me with your eyes in Jesus Christ's name (Ps 32:28)

13. I will sleep well, I will not be kept awake by any spirit of restlessness in Jesus Christ's name (Ps 3:5)

14. I quench with the shield of faith every fiery dart the enemy sends my way (Eph 6:16)

15. Lord I nullify and destroy every dream sent from hell to altar your destiny for my life.

16. Oh Lord arise and put and end to constant disappointments in my life and ministry

17. Lord, let shame and reproach be the lot of those who are out to bring shame and reproach in my life

18. I destroy every evil satanic program to stop the original plan and purpose of God for my life in Jesus' name

19. I cancel every satanic deposit brought into my life through dreams, to destroy the entire original plan and purpose of God in the name of Jesus Christ of Nazareth.

20. By my own will every covenant made by my ancestors that has kept me behind in life, I break it in the mighty name of Jesus Christ.

21. You strange spirit trying to destroy the original plan and purpose of God for my life receive fire in the name of Jesus Christ name.

# Chapter 10

# The Mystery Blood Covenant

## Meaning of Blood

The red fluid that is pumped through the body by the heart and contains plasma blood cells, and platelets. Blood carries oxygen and nutrients to the tissues and carries away waste products.

Blood is the only liquid that breathes and cries "your brother's blood cries out to you from the ground" (Gen 4:10). The blood of Jesus is the most powerful blood. It has brought salvation, healing and redemption. The scriptures explain that if the blood of bulls and goats were able to safe, then the Blood of Jesus which is superior to any other blood can save. Jesus used His Blood to sign a new and better covenant. "And to Jesus the Mediator of the new covenant, and the blood of sprinkling, that speaketh better things than that of Abel."

The first blood that Jesus shed was on the 8th day after His birth. According to Jewish custom he was circumcised on the 8th day and His first Blood was shed.

Another important thing is the application of the blood by faith such as taking the communion. Since life is in the blood, we will behave like Christ when we take the communion. This is why the Bible tells us not eat an animal with the blood in it so that we don't behave like that animal. The blood is also for atonement. That means the Blood of Jesus pays for any debt that you owe in the spiritual realm. What words cannot do the Blood of Jesus will do it. The Blood of Jesus performs many miracles. The Blood of Jesus is a settlement card. Let's examine more of those miracles the Blood of Jesus does.

**Forgiveness of Sins**

"Whom God set forth as propitiation by His Blood through faith to demonstrate His righteousness because in his forbearance God had Passover our sins that was previously committed." (Rom 3:25)

God appointed Jesus to shed His Blood to forgive our past sins as long as we accept Him as Lord. His death broke the power of sin over our lives. His death also brought peace and bridges the gulf between man and

God and stored broken relationship between man and God. Christ's death on the cross showed that there was no salvation by the Law.

One day a prostitute attended a church service on a Good Friday. After the service, she approached the pastor and asked if she also could be forgiven because according to her she had destroyed many marriages through her sexual behavior. Men have divorced their legal wives because of her relationship with those men. The preacher told her that she has been forgiven as long as she confesses and that when God forgives he forgets and referred her to Isaiah 43:25 which says, "I, even I, I am he who blots out your transgressions for my own sake, And I will not remember your sins." One thing God hates is to continue sinning and repenting.

**Healings of Sicknesses**

Another mystery of the Blood of Jesus is the healing we receive through the Blood of Jesus. Isaiah, the prophet puts it in this way, "Surely he borne our grief. And carried our sorrows, yet we esteem him stricken smitten by God, and afflicted. But he was wounded for our transgression; He was wounded for our iniquities. The chastisement for peace was upon Him and by his stripes we are healed." (Isaiah 53:4-5)

His feet were nailed to the cross and he bled. The blood on his feet set us free from any bondage and antiprogress, stagnation, limitation witchcraft and retrogression. The blood has washed and cleansed our feet. Therefore, wherever our feet touch we are supposed to take possession. Any sickness on our feet we are to claim our healing through the nails on his feet.

We received healings from the blood that came from his side. Therefore any sickness in any part of our side is healed through the blood. The soldiers pierced his side. Blood and water came out. The water stands for Holy Spirit. Through his hands, nailed to the cross, his hands bled. The blood that came from his hands releases us from poverty and blesses the work of our hands. There was also crown thorn on his head. The crown bruised his face all over. The blood was shed to remove shame and give us glory that God originally gave to us. Finally, Jesus' life changed the criminal on the cross to accept Christ. Receiving healing in any part of our physical and spiritual body is a mystery.

**Justified**

"And since we have been made right in God's sight by the blood of Jesus Christ, He will certainly keep us from Gods' condemnation. For since our friendship with God was restored by the death of his son while we were still enemies, we will certainly be saved through the life of his son." (NKJ). (Rom 5:9-10)

Paul says through Christ's death, we are justified into God's spiritual family. This means we have right relationship with God. Adam's sin was a sentence of death when we were considered as sinners. Jesus offered himself as a gift of salvation because of the love he had for humankind.

The same love that caused Christ to die is the same love that sends the Holy Spirit to live in us and guide us daily. Be assured that having begun a new life with Christ we have power and love to call on him each day for help to meet every challenge or trial. God is holy and does not associate with sin. Our sinful nature separated us from the Lord but Christ has bridged the gap. All sins deserve punishments with the death we deserve. However, Christ took our sins upon himself and took our punishments by going on the cross. Through our faith in Christ's work on the cross, we become God's friends rather than being enemies and outcasts. For one persons blood to get the whole world freedom is a mystery.

**Redemption**

Paul has this to say in this scripture, "He is so rich in kindness and grace that he purchased our freedom with the blood of his son and forgave us our sins" (Eph 1:7)

Redemption was the price paid to gain freedom for a slave to sin. In Old Testament times forgiveness was granted based on the shedding of blood. We are, therefore, forgiven based on the basis of the shedding of Christ's blood. Jesus died as the final and perfect sacrifice.

Peter confirms what Paul states above that if the blood of animals could save us from empty, vain, foolish and unprofitable things than certain the precious blood of Christ care save our souls from death. It is only the blood of Jesus that can pay for anything in the spirit world. The effects of sin which included sickness, pain, suffering death were part of the curse. These things removed us from God's plan for us. The Blood has removed those curses. We no longer have to live in sin again.

## Sanctification

"And from Jesus Christ, the faithful witness the first born from the dead, and ruler over the kings of the earth. To him who loved us and washed us from our sins in his own blood". (Rev. 1:5)

The word sanctification simply means to cleanse or make holy. It's the process by which we become partners of God's holiness according to his will. Justification refers to a judicial act of God whereby believers are once assured of all their guilt and accounted legally righteous. Sanctification is a progress work right from the time one is born again. It is carried on in the hearts of believers by the presence of the Holy Spirit. When we become Christians, God expects us to be holy as Peter states, "you shall be Holy as I am holy" (1 Peter 1:16). Christ is our sanctification. He used his blood to make sure we are cleansed according to Paul in Colossian 1:30. Paul refers to Christians as the "holy ones" in Romans 1:7 to mean that sanctification is the possession of believers.

In the Old Testament, God revealed himself to Moses as the God who sanctifies Jehova-Makkedash in Exodus 19.

**Reconciliation**

"For God was in the Christ reconciling the world to him no longer counting peoples sins against them. And he gave us this wonderful message of reconciliation". (2 Cor 5:19)

Paul explains here that God brings us back to himself by blotting out our sings and making us right with him. When we trust God we are no longer God's enemies, or strangers or foreigners to him. Since we are reconciled to God we, need to encourage others to come to Christ. We have the duty to reconcile others to Christ. This is mystery because the blood the power to bring us back to God as friend again.

Our forefathers used the blood of animals to reconcile a man and wife or any two partners they had problems. The shedding of the blood of animals brought two parties together again. In the some vein the blood Jesus has given us the access to the throne of grace as Hebrew 9:12 explains.

**Protection**

On that night I will pass through the land of Egypt. I will execute Judgment against and the gods of Egypt, for I am the Lord. But the blood on your door posts will serve as a sign making the houses where you are staying when I see the blood I will pass over you. This plague of death will lust towards you when I smite the gods of Egypt. (Exodus 12:12-13)

God said that for the Israelites to be spared from placed on the door frames of each home of the Israelites.

In killing the lamb, the Israelites shed innocent blood. The lamb was a sacrifice a substitute for the person who the lamb was sacrifice, a substitutes for the person who will have died in the plague. The Hebrew was made to understand that for them to be spared from death an innocent life had to be sacrificed in their place. The name for Passover in Hebrew is "Pesach" which simply means to "Passover". This is the first feast established by God for the Israelites and was asked to observe it as an ordinance forever. God sent Hs final and most powerful plague- the killing of the firstborn male in every home in Egypt.

In Exodus 12:7 God instructed the people of Israel to apply the blood to their door posts in new specific manner. He said they were to apply it to the sides and the top of the door were left with the letter" "Chet": which is the 8th letter in the Hebrew alphabet. It carries the meaning of life. When the angel of death came to a house that had the letter of life on it, it had to Passover the house that had the life on it. Death could not where life was placed life. **Now** that God lives in your death cannot touch you.

As believers, we need to apply the blood of Jesus over our marriages, our children, love ones and our businesses. As long as by faith we apply the blood to the door posts of our homes, the enemy cannot and will not attempt to come by. Every time we face an attack or difficult circumstances, just turn to the life giving blood of the lamb had to be applied personally on the door posts in every home. We also by faith, must apply the blood of the sacrifice of Jesus when applied in faith protects us from every attack of the enemy. There is power in the blood of made by our ancestors or by us knowingly or unknowingly. The blood of Jesus supersedes any currency in the spiritual realm. Therefore, used o pay for any debt that you owe

## Defeats the Devil

"Having disarmed principalities and powers, he made a public spectacle of them triumphing over them in it" (Colossians 2:15).

In this scripture, Paul explains how Christ's death and resurrection has disarmed Satan and his demons, false idols of pagan religious evil world governments. This public show of disarming is like stripping a defeated enemy of an armor on the battlefield. Evil no longer has any power over believers because Christ has disarmed it.

This is why Paul said in Colossian 1:13 that, "He has rescued us from the kingdom of darkness and transferred us into the kingdom of dear son". As children of the Most High Christ has already defeated Satan and his agents.

Therefore, we have every right to kick him out of our marriages our financiers, church and our children's lives. This is mystery for the Blood shed two thousand years ago and still able to defeat the devil of every attack on our lives. By faith let's apply the blood against every attack of the enemy.

# About the Author

In February, 1989 Rev. Dr Emmanuel Oduro had a Divine Revelation in which he was Privileged to see the Day of the Lord. It was a terrible sight, as everyone was running and weeping for help. In a second visitation, the Lord asked him to testify of what had been revealed to him earlier. For about five years, Emmanuel ran away from the call of God until January 1994, when he surrendered. He began to prepare himself for ministry by enrolling at Tyndale University College and Seminary in Toronto. His formal theological studies were enhanced by practical spiritual training from Prophet Roger Winnepeg, Dr. David Sherbino, Late Apostle E.K. Owusu and a twenty-one-day encounter with the Lord at Mount Horeb Prayer Camp, which paved the way for full-time ministry. He also holds a BA from York University, Toronto. In May 2000, Dr Oduro was ordained by the Evangelical Church Alliance of United States. He is currently the

Senior Pastor of Good News International Church in Toronto. Dr. Oduro is a dynamic minister of the gospel who provides in-depth teaching of the powerful Word of God. As he ministers, the power of the Holy Spirit moves through him to prophesy, edify and uplift. The Lord speaks through him with personal words of wisdom and encouragement. He is known as a teacher of teachers. He has traveled with the Gospel to several parts of the world. He conducts seminars for church leaders especially in Canada and the U.S. Dr Emmanuel Oduro is married to his lovely and devoted wife Helena, who is a constant source of love and support to him in ministry. Mama Helena's humility and genuine love for God has led to her counseling program for abuse women called D.I.V.A. Café. She has committed herself in bringing up their four handsome boys, Kwame, Samuel, David and Daniel in the ways of the Lord.